ColourScene
The Vehicles of
East Kent and Maidstone & District
Volume Two
1986 - 1997

N. J. Eadon-Clarke

DTS Publishing

Published: 2006
ISBN: 1-900515-31-8
Published by: DTS Publishing, PO Box 105, Croydon, UK
Printed by: Ian Allan Printing Limited, Hersham KT12 4RG
© N. J.Eadon-Clarke 2006

DTS Publishing   *www.BooksDTS.co.uk*

COVER PICTURES:

FRONT: Representing the high standard of the East Kent fleet is MK2 Metrobus 7755. Although over 5 years old the smart livery enhances the quality feel. It stands in Pencester Road Dover. **5 June 1993**

BACK: Maidstone & District Leyland Olympian 5942 new in April carries dedicated paint work for the Maidstone to Chatham trunk route 101 seen here at Gillingham bus station. **16 August 1997**

FRONTISPIECE: The oldest surviving complete East Kent bus is JG669, built in 1930 it is a Tilling-Stevens B10C2 with Brush B37R body. Seen here taking a break in Crawley during its participation on the annual HCVS London to Brighton Road Run. It won the Charles W Banfield Challenge Cup for the best restoration during the past year by a Society member of limited means. **4 May 1986**

THIS PAGE:

UPPER: In 1983 East Kent embarked on a programme of re-bodying a batch of ten 1974 AEC Reliances. The first vehicle treated, following major accident damage was HFN28L, which, seen here with its new Berkhof Esprite C49F body became 8197. It is pictured in the village of Leeds near Maidstone. These rebodied vehicles had a relatively short life in the fleet due to their being under-powered with the new, heavier, bodies. This particular vehicle spent its entire career at Folkestone. **17 May 1986**

LOWER: As a direct consequence of de-regulation in October 1986 large quantities of minibuses entered service throughout the UK. Maidstone & District used the Mercedes Benz L608D as their 'standard'. Here 1003 stands at the rear of Chatham garage prior to entering service in July at Sittingbourne. **17 May 1986**

ColourScene
The Vehicles of
East Kent and Maidstone & District
Volume Two
1986 -1997

Foreword

This book starts at a time when the companies were facing a period of major uncertainty on two main fronts. It had been announced by the Government that the NBC subsidiaries would be sold from late 1986 and in addition de-regulation of bus services would take place from 26 October 1986. To allow for de-regulation the companies were required to register all services that they planned to operate commercially (ie. without subsidy) from 26 October 1986 by 28 February to allow time for local authorities to prepare tender documents for other services considered necessary for social need and offer them to all operators in open competition. The major NBC companies were all fearful of local competition in the de-regulated market and in order to counter this threat embarked on a programme to introduce minibuses to areas such as large housing estates where the roads were unsuitable for full size buses in the hope that this would increase their own market share and prevent smaller operators targeting areas not traditionally served hitherto. Maidstone & District and Hastings and District were allocated the Mercedes-Benz L608D as the basis of their minibuses whereas East Kent had examples based on both the Ford Transit and Freight Rover Sherpa. Another consequence of the future uncertainty was the lack of new investment in vehicles (other than minibuses), however both companies took particular advantage of the sell-off of surplus vehicles by Greater Manchester Buses and also took other suitable mid life vehicles to meet their changing requirements. The book finishes in 1997 by which time the ownership and operations had become much more stable.

Some of the key dates during this period are as follows:

EAST KENT

March 1987	Privatised by a management buy-out
November 1987	The assets of Marinair are acquired
September 1993	Sold to Stagecoach Holdings PLC

MAIDSTONE & DISTRICT

November 1986	Privatised by a management buy-out
June 1988	The assets of New Enterprise Coaches acquired
December 1991	The Tunbridge Wells local bus operations of Shearings are acquired
June 1992	The assets of Boro'line are acquired (less the tendered LT services)
May 1994	The local bus operations of Bygone buses are absorbed
April 1995	Sold to British Bus
May 1996	The former Grey Green local routes were acquired from London Coaches (Kent)
July 1996	British Bus bought by Cowie
September 1996	The assets of Mercury Passenger Services are acquired

HASTINGS & DISTRICT

November 1987	Privatised by a management buy-out
December 1989	Sold to Stagecoach Holdings PLC

I have used various publications published by The Maidstone & District and East Kent Bus Club for details in this book and accordingly wish to record my thanks for their permission to do so. Membership of the club is highly recommended and details may be found on page 96. I am grateful to Nicholas King for proof-reading the text and making appropriate suggestions which I have incorporated where possible; any remaining errors are mine. In addition I would like to thank Mike Davis of DTS Publishing who has provided much help particularly with regards to content and layout and everything else needed to enable this book to reach the book shelves.

I hope you enjoy this collection of East Kent, Maidstone & District and Hastings & District vehicles which illustrates an interesting period of changing ownership, liveries and vehicle operations.

Nigel Eadon-Clarke   June 2006
Chislehurst
Kent
UK

LEFT: Davian Coaches of Enfield are using this former East Kent AEC Regent V WFN831 new in 1961. This Regent was delivered with an offside illuminated advertisement panel, evidence of which can still be seen in this view at the Davian operating centre. **10 May 1986**

LEFT: In order to celebrate the 75th anniversary of Maidstone & District Bristol VRT 5857 received traditional livery in spring 1986 together with suitable displays on the front and sides. It is seen here at Chatham railway station on route 101 which links Chatham and Maidstone. **17 May 1986**

LEFT: Delivered new in July 1973 as Maidstone & District 4112 (4xxx denoting full coach specification) this Leyland Leopard with Duple C44F body was renumbered as 2112 in the dual purpose and OMO coach category in 1983. It carries Invictaway livery outside Gillingham garage, having been reseated to accommodate 49 in December 1981. **17 May 1986**

ABOVE LEFT: New in January 1979 Maidstone & District Leyland Leopard 2149 with a Duple Dominant I Express body incorporating a blind display above the windscreen (compare with previous photo of 2112) on the forecourt of Gillingham garage. **17 May 1986**

ABOVE RIGHT: Sharing the rear yard of Maidstone & District Chatham (Luton) garage with former LT DM 1718 is Metrobus 5270, one of a batch of five with various different engine and brake combinations delivered in 1980 as part of trials for NBC. This bus had a Rolls Royce 'Eagle' engine and air brakes. **17 May 1986**

BELOW: Maidstone & District who were already an operator of Dennis Dominators acquired new, took the opportunity to acquire further second hand vehicles including several from the fleet of East Staffordshire District Council when they were bought by Stevensons of Uttoxeter. M&D 5315 was acquired carrying this overall advertisement livery for Ind Coope a famous Burton-on-Trent brewery and entered service in this condition. It is parked in the rear yard of Chatham (Luton) garage. **17 May 1986**

BOTTOM RIGHT: Originally with East Kent RFN967G was acquired by Maidstone & District in 1983, following a 'tidying-up' exercise between the M&D and East Kent fleets. Standing in the front yard of Chatham (Luton) garage in full NBC livery. The addition of wording under the fleetname to mark 75 years of M&D operation can be seen. **17 May 1986**

BELOW: A line of three former London Transport DMS class Daimler Fleetlines now in the fleet of Maidstone & District at the rear of Chatham (Luton) garage. These had been acquired in 1982 and were originally DMS2066, DM1737 & DMS1947 now numbered 5026, 5025 and 5035. DM1737 would be involved in an accident in 1988 and its stock number would be re-assigned to former DM1830 acquired with the business of New Enterprise and illustrated later in this book. **17 May 1986**

LEFT: In common with all other parts of the country de-regulation in 1986 saw a substantial growth in the use of the minibus which was seen as a useful 'tool' to penetrate areas unsuitable for full size buses and at the same time discourage competition from smaller operators, or to sustain routes unprofitable with bigger buses. Maidstone & District used the Mercedes Benz L608D as its 'standard' minibus. Here is the first 1001 which poses for the camera at Gillingham garage, the body by Rootes was a conversion from a panel van as evidenced by the indentations on the window pillars. **17 May 1986**

ABOVE: Maidstone & District Bristol VRT 6682 was built to the lowest height (13'5"), originally for use in the Hastings area, as can be evidenced by the lack of the central white band on the front. It is leaving Borough Green garage en route to Maidstone. This bus would be withdrawn later in the year and transferred to the service vehicle fleet as a towing bus. **17 May 1986**

LEFT: Intermediate or standard height VRT (13'8") Maidstone & District 5828 stands at Borough Green garage. After withdrawal in 1990 this bus would give many more years service with Ham of Flimwell. **17 May 1986**

LEFT: Maidstone & District service vehicle P33 PFN865 was converted from a former East Kent AEC Regent V. As seen here at Borough Green garage it operated on Trade Plates in its new role as a recovery vehicle. It is now preserved in this form in Nottingham. **17 May 1986**

BELOW: In order to replace a fire damaged vehicle Maidstone & District acquired this Leyland Leopard with Duple Dominant II coachwork from Golden Boy of Roydon in 1983. It was numbered 4771 to match its registration plate. It is parked inside Tunbridge Wells garage. **17 May 1986**

BOTTOM LEFT: East Kent received this AEC Reliance new with Park Royal body in 1962. In 1972 it received this new Plaxton Panorama body. Now in the fleet of Essex based Bordacoach, 524 FN was being displayed at the annual Southend bus rally. **1 June 1986**

BOTTOM RIGHT: Former East Kent AEC Swift VJG190J with Marshall B51F body is now in the fleet of Crusader Coaches although it is seen here in the yard of Don's of Dunmow. **7 June 1986**

LEFT: A tour of Essex and Suffolk by the M&D and East Kent Bus Club saw the hiring of this coach (511SKM) from the fleet of River Valley Coaches. It was new to East Kent as WJG141J and is seen here at Don's of Dunmow. **7 June 1986**

LEFT: New to Maidstone & District in 1974 as 5820 this Bristol VRT would have an eventful life. It had already served with Hastings & District before reaching its current owner Cambus in whose yard it is seen. It would go on to serve with several other operators. Note that the original green paint shows through where the side advertisement has been removed. **7 June 1986**

BELOW: Originally with East Kent this 1959 Park Royal bodied full front AEC Regent V PFN868 made this appearance at the annual North Weald bus rally. **22 June 1986**

LEFT: This standard height Bristol VRT numbered 7659 in the East Kent fleet is seen operating in Whitstable. **16 August 1986**

BELOW: This new to Southdown Daimler Fleetline now numbered 7326 in the East Kent fleet has been repainted to operate the Canterbury City Tour. In 1985 it operated without some upper deck windows, but these have now been refitted to allow operation through Canterbury West Gate. It poses for the camera in the yard of Herne Bay garage. **16 August 1986**

ABOVE: Also in Whitstable is East Kent Leyland National 1514 which had been new to Maidstone & District as their 3514. **16 August 1986**

RIGHT: Despite being 13 years old East Kent 1174 is still going strong. EFN174L was from the first batch of Leyland Nationals delivered to East Kent. Seen here at Herne Bay garage. **16 August 1986**

RIGHT: East Kent adopted this 'modern' interpretation of their original livery, Bristol VRT 7670 demonstrates the new scheme in Canterbury bus station. The underline stripes have been abbreviated following accident repairs. **16 August 1986**

RIGHT: In contrast to the plain NBC livery of surrounding vehicles in Canterbury bus station Willowbrook bodied Bristol VRT 7020 makes a fine sight in the new scheme. **16 August 1986**

BELOW LEFT: General view of the parking lay-over area within Canterbury bus station including Leyland National 1089 in dual purpose livery behind standard 1120. **16 August 1986**

BELOW RIGHT: The Isle of Thanet open top route 69 sees 'Viking Glory' former Maidstone & District Leyland Atlantean 572RKJ now re-registered by East Kent to XKO72A. The new registration has not caused a fleet number change and it remains 0572. Caught by the camera at Broadstairs. **16 August 1986**

LEFT: Preserved 1959 Park Royal full fronted AEC Regent V PFN874 makes a fine sight as it stands outside Thanet (Westwood) garage in the summer sunshine. **16 August 1986**

CENTRE LEFT: In 1986 East Kent acquired a batch of twelve 1974 Park Royal bodied Leyland Atlanteans from Northern General. Here OTY412M, RCN107N and PCN893N await attention in the yard of Thanet (Westwood) garage, they would all enter service in October, however repaints stretched from September '86 to January '87, some entering service with East Kent fleet names before repainting. **16 August 1986**

BELOW LEFT: Underneath these embellishments is East Kent AEC Regent V PFN873. This had operated in open top form on the Thanet open top route, but has now become the 'carnival bus'. Its original registration plate has already been transferred to a MCW Metroliner coach and as can be seen it now carries XKO41A. It is parked inside Thanet (Westwood) garage. **16 August 1986**

BELOW RIGHT: Two East Kent coaches inside Thanet (Westwood) garage both carrying blind displays for Day-Break Tours, on the left is 8558 a 12 metre long AEC Reliance with Duple Dominant C53F body delivered new in 1975 and standing next to it is 8848 the first of the 1984 batch of MCW Metroliners carrying National Holidays livery. This second batch of Metroliners had a revised front compared to the initial batch illustrated elsewhere in this book. **16 August 1986**

ABOVE LEFT: Showing full NBC poppy red livery is 7963 a 1969 Daimler Fleetline with Park Royal body in its last year with the company. It is working Thanet route 51 when captured opposite Thanet (Westwood) garage. **16 August 1986**

ABOVE RIGHT: This view in the yard of Thanet (Westwood) garage shows East Kent Daimler Fleetline 7962 parked next to two recently acquired ex Northern General Atlanteans (RCN110N and RCN100N). **16 August 1986**

CENTRE LEFT: A low bridge accident in 1981 when it was only three years old caused the open top conversion of East Kent Willowbrook bodied Bristol VRT RVB977S seen here at Thanet (Westwood) garage. **16 August 1986**

LEFT: The East Kent open top fleet consisted of three vehicles, in addition to the Bristol VRT were these two former Maidstone & District Leyland Atlanteans, both now re-registered. XKO72A was new as 572RKJ and XKO54A was new as 620UKM, they pose for the camera outside their home Thanet (Westwood) garage. **16 August 1986**

ABOVE: The former toll bridge in Sandwich makes an interesting backdrop for this view of East Kent Bristol VRT open topper 0977 during a club tour. **16 August 1986**

RIGHT: New to LCBS as LNB67 this Leyland National is now 1067 in the East Kent fleet and operating from Dover garage on Sealink services between the docks and Dover Priory railway station. In order to accommodate passengers' luggage this has been converted internally and now has only 30 seats. **16 August 1986**

BELOW LEFT: Standing opposite Dover garage East Kent Leyland National 1165 shows the new livery to good effect. **16 August 1986**

BELOW RIGHT: Not all the ex LCBS Leyland Nationals carried Sealink livery. In standard NBC livery at Pencester Road Dover we find NPD151L which is now 1151 in the East Kent fleet. **16 August 1986**

RIGHT: Carrying '1066' colorbus livery is this Bristol VRT in the Hastings & District fleet. 522 was new to Maidstone & District as 5122 seen here in Pencester Road Dover. **16 August 1986**

BELOW LEFT: In 1985 Maidstone & District acquired three Willowbrook "Spacecar 008" bodied Leyland Leopards from Ribble Motor Services. 4139 is seen at Bossington Road near Adisham while on hire to the M&D and East Kent Bus Club. **16 August 1986**

BELOW RIGHT: East Kent's first batch of 26 Leyland Nationals were received in 1972/3. Here 1183 the penultimate member is working route 621 en route to Canterbury when seen at Bossington Road Adisham. **16 August 1986**

BOTTOM: This view outside Norwich castle shows former Maidstone & District Bristol highbridge VRT 5731 which is now Eastern Counties HVR 331. The broad centre yellow band and yellow roof provide a visual distinction of the vehicle's height compared to the standard ECOC VRT which were all lower. **2 September 1986**

14

ABOVE LEFT: Maidstone & District minibus 1015 stands in Sittingbourne town centre having entered service in June 1986. **25 October 1986**

ABOVE RIGHT: The Hastings & District fleet received their Mercedes minibuses with Alexander bodies, this vehicle numbered 848 was one of six fitted with high backed coach seats which reduced their internal capacity by one to 19. It stands at Hastings cricket ground. **3 January 1987**

LEFT: Typical of several H&D minibuses that ran for some months in white before receiving fleet livery is No. 832 in the town centre. **3 January 1987**

BELOW: Canterbury bus station is the setting for East Kent Bristol VRT wearing this all over advertisement livery for the 'Field and Trek' shop in Canterbury. **2 May 1987**

ABOVE: The initial minibuses for East Kent were based on both the Ford Transit and the Freight Rover. Here four Freight Rover Sherpas line up in Canterbury, No.36 heads the line with 45, 38 and an unidentified fourth behind. **2 May 1987**

ABOVE LEFT: This view of East Kent Sherpa minibus 38 taken at the terminus in Canterbury shows the sliding entrance door for the driver. **2 May 1987**

ABOVE RIGHT: A rear view of East Kent Sherpa minibus 45 in Canterbury showing the positioning of rear advertising. **2 May 1987**

LEFT: Acquired from Devon General the previous year is Bristol VRT MOD570P now East Kent 7570. Alongside in Canterbury bus station is Leyland National 1121 both in the new livery. **2 May 1987**

LEFT: P35, the recovery truck at Gillingham garage of Maidstone & District is seen here at its home base. This vehicle was acquired from Gulf Oil in 1979 and whilst operated on trade plates was actually registered MMK502L. **2 May 1987**

BELOW: New to London Transport as DMS2087 this bus is now 5029 in the Maidstone & District fleet. It stands in the Chatham Pentagon bus station before departing on route 136 to Gravesend. **2 May 1987**

BOTTOM: In order to promote the developments in the former Naval Dockyard at Chatham, Maidstone & District Leyland National 3547 was given this all over advertisement livery for Chatham Maritime, it is about to enter the entrance ramp for Chatham Pentagon bus station. **2 May 1987**

RIGHT: National Holidays liveried East Kent Metroliner 8845 from the first batch enters Chatham Pentagon bus station. **2 May 1987**

BELOW LEFT: The small fleet number of 8520 identifies this as a former East Kent AEC Reliance seen in the yard of dealer Wealden at Five Oak Green. **16 May 1987**

BELOW RIGHT: Moss covered former Maidstone & District Leyland Panther LKT132F in the yard of Wealden, Five Oak Green. This would be returned to full glory in preservation and is illustrated as such later in this book. **16 May 1987**

BELOW: Club transport for the day was provided by Maidstone & District Leyland Leopard 2170 with its distinctive ECW body. It stands in the entrance to the yard of Wealden at Five Oak Green. **16 May 1987**

LEFT: Maidstone & District Leyland Leopard 3456 with Marshall B52F body seen at work in Tunbridge Wells. This was one of a few in this batch that were upseated from 45 with 3+2 seating. This programme was abandoned because of service cuts and the modified vehicles were disposed of prematurely. **16 May 1987**

CENTRE LEFT: The village of Penshurst is the setting for Maidstone & District Leyland Leopard 2838 with Willowbrook 003 MK II dual purpose bodywork in Invictaway livery on Saturday-only route 232 via Chiddingstone Causeway, en route to Edenbridge. **16 May 1987**

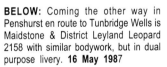

BELOW: Coming the other way in Penshurst en route to Tunbridge Wells is Maidstone & District Leyland Leopard 2158 with similar bodywork, but in dual purpose livery. **16 May 1987**

LEFT: Resting inside the Edenbridge garage of Maidstone & District we find two Leyland Leopards. 3459 and 3452 had both been new in 1972 and would each serve the company for over 20 years before disposal. **16 May 1987**

BELOW: Not what it seems; the registration plate only from East Kent AEC Reliance 536FN now adorns a coach previously registered SVF511W in the fleet of Cobham Hire Services of Norfolk, it passes the London Country garage at Northfleet. **31 May 1987**

LEFT: Caught in traffic in Ashford is Maidstone & District 5783 one of the East Lancs bodied Bristol VRTs acquired from South Yorkshire PTE in 1980, it would be sold for scrap in May 1988. **13 June 1987**

ABOVE: Compare the old and new liveries on this pair of Leyland Nationals parked in the yard of Ashford garage. The older vehicle 1503 in the new livery was acquired from Maidstone & District in 1983 and was one of that Company's initial five such vehicles. 1340 was a 10.3metre 1974 delivery to East Kent. **13 June 1987**

RIGHT: Two East Kent Ford Transit minibuses in Folkestone bus station, on the left is 25 with Dormobile B16F body, next to it is 79 based on the revised Ford Transit model showing the new frontal design, this bus was diverted to East Kent from South Midland Ltd and was a replacement for Sherpa 30 which was written off after an accident in January 1987. **13 June 1987**

BELOW: Standing outside Dover garage is East Kent 8201 in National Holidays livery. The AEC Reliance chassis was new in 1973 as HFN27L and the new Berkhof body was fitted in 1984. **13 June 1987**

LEFT: Looking somewhat down at heel is East Kent Daimler Fleetline 7325 at the Dover Pencester Road parking area. This was one of 13 similar vehicles acquired from Southdown Motor Services in 1981.
13 June 1987

LEFT: East Kent Leyland Tiger 8841 with Plaxton Paramount 3200 body seating 53 shows off the National Express livery in Pencester Road Dover.
13 June 1987

LEFT: The blind layout on this Northern Counties bodied Leyland Atlantean immediately identifies this bus as originating with Greater Manchester PTE. Now East Kent 7178, GDB178N was new in 1975 and this was one of 10 similar vehicles recently acquired. It entered East Kent service only a couple of days prior to this shot of it passing Thanet (Westwood) garage on route 51A. Later in this book (July 1994) it can be seen after sale by East Kent.
13 June 1987

RIGHT: 1967 East Kent AEC Regent V MFN943F received traditional East Kent livery in 1984 to mark the 25th anniversary of the first Regent Vs bought by East Kent and was pictured when first repainted in the previous volume. It was also the last East Kent Regent used in passenger service on 12 March 1987 and it was then used for a few weeks as a trainer. It is shown here withdrawn outside Thanet (Westwood) garage awaiting its fate. **13 June 1987**

RIGHT: Also awaiting disposal at Thanet (Westwood) garage is this former Southdown Daimler Fleetline. 7206 was one of several 'PUF' registered Fleetlines acquired, some of the others carried Hoverspeed colours. **13 June 1987**

RIGHT: East Kent Fleetline 7965 next to a former GMPTE Atlantean at Thanet (Westwood) garage. The square 'EK' sticker has been applied to cover the NBC 'arrows' although 18 years old it still looks to be in good condition. **13 June 1987**

LEFT: Willowbrook bodied Bristol VRT 7986 in the East Kent fleet seen at work in Camber. **15 August 1987**

LEFT: Hastings & District Bristol VRT 530 with ECW highbridge body stands on the forecourt of Rye garage. This special livery was generally confined to vehicles based at Rye at this time. **15 August 1987**

LEFT: Hastings & District 466 is a Bristol RESL acquired from Ribble for schools work at Rye in 1986, the paint scheme is described as Regency Cream and Brilliant Red seen here at Rye station. **15 August 1987**

RIGHT: Another vehicle acquired from Ribble by Hastings & District, but this time in 1984 is Leyland National 253. This bus is adaptable to B24F with a central lift and the ability to carry wheelchairs. It poses for the camera outside Rye garage. **15 August 1987**

RIGHT: Maidstone & District acquired 12 of these Bristol VRTs with East Lancs bodywork from South Yorkshire PTE in 1980 and in May 1983 five were transferred to Hastings & District, represented here by 571 in this newly introduced livery. By 1987 only this one remained in the H&D fleet. It stands at Rye station outside the garage. **15 August 1987**

RIGHT: Hastings & District highbridge Bristol VRT 524 was new to Maidstone & District in 1976 and transferred in 1983, seen here outside Rye garage. **15 August 1987**

LEFT: This is 'Alice' and was acquired for private hire work from Linden-Bull of Melksham in 1985. Also used for round the town tours of Hastings in inclement weather. Registered CHL772 it is a Daimler CVD6 with Willowbrook DP35F bodywork seen outside Rye garage. **15 August 1987**

LEFT: Hastings & District coach, with fleet number 171, was originally registered FKL171Y with Maidstone & District, and was 'on hire' from them from December 1983 before being acquired in February 1985. Seen here in National Holidays livery in Hastings (Silverhill) garage yard. **15 August 1987**

BELOW: A magnificent view of vintage vehicles still in regular use in Hastings. The two open top AEC Regals date from 1946 (HKL826) and 1947 (HKL836) and the Daimler from 1949. They are parked for the camera in the yard of Hastings (Silverhill) garage. Happily all three vehicles still exist with other owners in 2006. **15 August 1987**

RIGHT: The Hastings & District mobile office AEC Regent V MFN946F was new to East Kent in 1967. It too survives in 2006 as a Heritage vehicle with East Kent. It is standing in Hastings (Silverhill) garage yard. **15 August 1987**

BELOW LEFT: Prior to placing an order for Iveco minibuses East Kent took this vehicle on demonstration but did not use it in service. D618BCK from the Ribble fleet, but carrying the livery of Alder Valley South from whom it was diverted is seen inside Ashford garage. **15 August 1987**

BELOW RIGHT: The initial batch of minibuses for Maidstone & District were based on the Mercedes L608D, but the next batch as illustrated here by 1050 outside Gillingham garage were based on the newer Mercedes 609D. **13 March 1988**

RIGHT: After privatisation Maidstone & District changed the white parts of its livery to cream as illustrated here by the long wheelbase Olympians outside Gillingham garage. 5443 and 5450 carrying the new scheme whilst 5441 has yet to be so treated. **13 March 1988**

LEFT: Maidstone & District Leyland Leopard 2834 carries a Willowbrook DP47F body. This attractive vehicle is seen on a gloomy day at Gillingham garage **13 March 1988**

LEFT: Maidstone & District also took advantage of the premature sale of mid life vehicles by Greater Manchester Buses and acquired fifteen Northern Counties bodied Leyland Atlanteans similar to 5727 seen here at Gillingham garage. Unlike East Kent M&D modified their destination display equipment before their entry into service. **13 March 1988**

LEFT: In 1972 fifty Leyland Atlantean Specials were diverted away from Midland Red. LCBS received thirty and numbered them AN91 - AN120. Maidstone & District received the other twenty as their 5701 – 5720. Eighteen were delivered between October and December 1972 and the last two (5717 & 5720) were received in January 1973. These two are parked at Gillingham garage with 5720 in fleet livery and 5717 which had high backed seats fitted for Invictaway services in dual purpose livery. Alongside is Long Wheelbase Invictaway Olympian 5442.
13 March 1988

RIGHT: In addition to Leyland National 3547 pictured earlier (2 May 1987), Maidstone & District painted minibus 1065 in a similar livery. It pauses in Gillingham bus station. **13 March 1988**

RIGHT: An overcast day sees Maidstone & District 2186 a Leyland Tiger with Plaxton Paramount 3500 3 C53F body in Maldon, Essex during a tour by the M&D and East Kent Bus Club. The coach was only two months old at this time. **18 June 1988**

RIGHT: On 22 June 1988 Einkorn Ltd the holding company of Maidstone & District purchased the assets of New Enterprise Coaches (Tonbridge) Ltd. Upon acquisition the New Enterprise double deck fleet consisted of one ex East Kent Regent V and seven ex LT DMS class Daimler Fleetlines. Two days after the change of ownership sees No.54 (DMS1614) at work at Tonbridge station still carrying the livery of its previous operator Keenan of Coalhall Ayrshire. This bus spent much of its LT life at Bromley garage and thus had almost come home after its life in Scotland. **24 June 1988**

RIGHT: East Kent usually send several vehicles to the Showbus rally which also had a reputation for rain. Here at Woburn Abbey is part of their 1988 offering. Bristol VRTs 7685 and 7022 carrying ECW and Willowbrook bodies respectively behind MK2 Metrobus 7750. **3 July 1988**

RIGHT: Also at the Showbus rally at Woburn Abbey is this ex Greater Manchester Buses Leyland Atlantean now 7553 in the East Kent fleet. **3 July 1988**

LEFT: Following successful trials East Kent purchased two batches of Robin Hood bodied Iveco minibuses in 1987. Here no 66 waits passengers in Ashford town centre. **30 July 1988**

LEFT: Delivered in February 1988 standard Mk 2 Metrobus 7748 is thus just five months old when captured on film working in Ashford. **30 July 1988**

LEFT: Canterbury bus station finds ex Northern General Park Royal bodied Leyland Atlantean 7108 between duties. **30 July 1988**

RIGHT: A pair of East Kent training buses in the lower shed of Ashford garage. On the left is P193 a 1967 AEC Regent V and next to it is P194 a 1973 Leyland National that had been new to Maidstone & District. **6 August 1988**

LEFT: In 1984 Maidstone & District received its first three standard Leyland Olympians which had been diverted from an order placed by Devon General. In December 1986 two were repainted into Invictaway livery as depicted here by 5890 outside Ashford garage. **6 August 1988**

RIGHT: Ricemans department store identifies this location as Canterbury bus station. Standard MK2 Metrobus 7750 is getting ready to leave on its next trip to Folkestone. **6 August 1988**

RIGHT: Ex Greater Manchester Buses Northern Counties bodied Leyland Atlantean HNB40N is now 7840 in the East Kent fleet and is seen loading up in Canterbury bus station. **6 August 1988**

ABOVE LEFT: East Kent Travel purchased the assets of Marinair Coach Services Ltd on 18 November 1987. Leyland National JJG904P was new to East Kent and hired to the Marinair fleet in June 1988. It is seen here in Marinair livery at Ramsgate Harbour. **6 August 1988**

ABOVE RIGHT: New to East Kent as No.70 E170UKR is also now on hire to the Marinair subsidiary and is depicted at work at Ramsgate harbour. **6 August 1988**

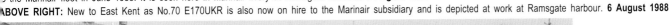

LEFT: In June 1987 earlier in this book I illustrated 7325 in service in Dover, here one year later it is withdrawn for disposal outside Thanet (Westwood) garage. **6 August 1988**

BELOW LEFT: East Kent already had a sizeable fleet of Metroliner single deck coaches and to add to their fleet purchased this former MCW demonstrator ABM399A in June 1988 after a period of hire. It was new in 1983 and originally registered A543WOB, it is parked inside Thanet (Westwood) garage and carries fleet number 8399. **6 August 1988**

BELOW RIGHT: Thanet (Westwood) garage entrance showing minibus 60 alongside two second hand Leyland Atlanteans, 7842 came from Greater Manchester Buses and 7110 came from Northern General and is illustrated in as acquired condition earlier in this book (August 1986). **6 August 1988**

ABOVE LEFT: Four single deck Metroliner coaches were acquired from Premier travel of Cambridge in spring 1988, after refurbishment by MCW B246JVA arrived with East Kent in June and was given East Kent fleet number 8246 which is just readable under the windscreen. It is seen at Thanet (Westwood) garage. **6 August 1988**

ABOVE RIGHT: East Kent 7411 an ex Northern Park Royal bodied Leyland Atlantean pauses opposite Thanet (Westwood) garage. The ex Northern Atlanteans were to have a short life with East Kent all being withdrawn by 1991. **6 August 1988**

LEFT: East Kent 7411 again, passing Marinair Bova Futura A513HBC in Broadstairs. **6 August 1988**

BELOW LEFT: Fifteen years old, but still looking good is East Kent Leyland National 1182 parked between journeys in Canterbury bus station. **6 August 1988**

BELOW RIGHT: Former East Kent AEC Regent V AFN778B is now with The Grand Garage a Peugeot / Talbot dealer it is seen in Cliftonville advertising its new owner, happily this bus is now preserved. **6 August 1988**

RIGHT: Still in NBC Poppy red East Kent Willowbrook bodied Bristol VRT 7018 stands in Canterbury bus station with 7023 behind carrying an all over advertisement for Glass (Canterbury) Ltd. **6 August 1988**

CENTRE RIGHT: East Kent Bristol VRT 7660 in an all over advertisement paint scheme for local Ford dealers Invicta Motors, the location is Canterbury bus station. **6 August 1988**

BELOW LEFT: Former Maidstone & District 3271 was from the second batch of Ford R1014 vehicles with Plaxton B43F bodywork. New in 1977 it was sold after only five years use and passed through a number of owners before being rescued from a scrap dealer in 1986 by Smith of Alcester in whose yard it is seen. It carries Dalesman of Ilkley livery to whom it had been on hire. **5 September 1988**

BELOW RIGHT: This 1973 Leyland Leopard had been refurbished by Maidstone & District and consequently was the last of its class. Originally numbered 4113 it later became 2113. Upon withdrawal in 1988 it passed to the New Enterprise subsidiary in June 1988 and received this attractive livery. It is pictured at its home base in Tonbridge. **20 May 1989**

35

ABOVE LEFT: One of several parking spots used by New Enterprise Coaches of Tonbridge finds AKP430T a Bedford YMT with Plaxton coach body next to former Maidstone & District Leyland Leopard 2160 which has bodywork by Willowbrook. **20 May 1989**

ABOVE RIGHT: At the time the newest vehicle in the New Enterprise fleet by some margin was C112AFX a Bedford YNV new to Excelsior of Bournemouth in 1986 seen at their Tonbridge yard. **20 May 1989**

LEFT: Two New Enterprise coaches that had been new to London Country Bus Services for Green Line work. Leyland Leopards MPL126W and MPL134W had both been acquired from Barrie of Alexandria in July 1988. Although they were both new in 1981 MPL126W had been re-bodied in 1983, they are parked at their Tonbridge base. **20 May 1989**

LEFT: Maidstone & District 2174 is a 1983 Leyland Tiger with Plaxton Paramount 3200 DP53F body. It is parked in Tunbridge Wells garage. **20 May 1989**

ABOVE: New in 1972 to Maidstone & District as 3457 this Leyland Leopard with Marshall body had been upseated to B52F by M&D in 1979 and was acquired by Wealden PSV in June 1988. It is seen here in Tunbridge Wells operating service 252 to Heathfield, this bus would later be exported to Malta for further service. **20 May 1989**

CENTRE RIGHT: Maidstone & District 5895 is a Leyland Olympian with Northern Counties body seen here in service in Tunbridge Wells. **20 May 1989**

RIGHT: In May 1987 Maidstone & District took over the operation of the replacement bus service from Tunbridge Wells to Groombridge following closure of Groombridge station. East Sussex County Council owned this Mercedes and it was accordingly transferred from the previous operator of the route; Tunbridge Wells Radio Taxis. It carried the M&D fleet number 1000 and it is seen in Tunbridge Wells. **20 May 1989**

LEFT: The sole Regent V in the fleet of New Enterprise is GJG750D seen here in Dartford on a club trip to South East London, it later passed to another Arriva company Leaside in North London and is now preserved. **20 May 1989**

RIGHT: Former London Transport Fleetline DM1090 is now P90 in the Maidstone & District Service vehicle fleet and was used in conjunction with the Network South East railway company as a bridge maintenance unit being used primarily to enable inspection of bridges that might have been damaged by road vehicles hitting their underside. This bus passed to M&D with the acquisition of New Enterprise Coaches, but was not used in normal service by M&D, instead it was converted for this role. It is seen in the railway yard of Norwood Junction Station. **26 May 1989**

ABOVE: Former East Kent Daimler Fleetline RFN961G was one of several from this batch that were acquired by the Guide Friday Sightseeing Company for operation in open top form on their Cambridge tour. It stands at the starting point of the tour, Cambridge railway station. **16 June 1989**

RIGHT: Another Fleetline from the East Kent fleet is RFN954G seen here with a full load on the Cambridge tour. **16 June 1989**

TOP: New in April East Kent Mk 2 Metrobus 7772 in the new livery seen opposite Thanet garage while working route 87 to Ramsgate. **5 July 1989**

ABOVE LEFT: Sister vehicle East Kent Metrobus Mk 2 7773 also delivered in April stands in a traffic free Margate on route 87. **5 July 1989**

ABOVE RIGHT: East Kent 7843 is an ex Greater Manchester Atlantean seen here in Margate working route 44. **5 July 1989**

LEFT: East Kent Mk 2 Metrobus 7765 is one of the batch of seven with coach seating also seen in Margate. **5 July 1989**

LEFT: Canterbury bus station finds East Kent Bristol VRT 7659 wearing this all over advertisement livery for the Chaucer Exhibition Centre **5 July 1989**

BELOW: Maidstone & District 2186 a Leyland Tiger new in 1988 with Plaxton "Paramount 3500 3" C53F bodywork is loading up outside Canterbury bus station. **5 July 1989**

BELOW LEFT: East Kent 8205 is a rebodied coach. The AEC Reliance chassis was new as HFN55L and was rebodied in 1984 emerging with this new Berkhof Esprite C49F body. Initially it carried "National Express Holiday" livery, but has now been repainted into the attractive East Kent livery seen here inside Dover garage. **22 July 1989**
BELOW RIGHT: Also inside Dover garage we find East Kent 8814 a Leyland Leopard with Duple Dominant II body new in 1980. **22 July 1989**

ABOVE: Former London Country NPD156L is now East Kent 1156. It is seen in Dover en route to the Eastern Docks in 'Sealink' livery with passengers travelling to Calais who will transfer at the ferry terminal onto a boat. **22 July 1989**

BELOW LEFT: Another former London Country Leyland National in use on connecting services for Sealink is NPD60L now East Kent 1060 also in Dover. **22 July 1989**

BELOW RIGHT: Top Line in Hastings was a joint venture between Southdown and Eastbourne Buses which competed with Hastings & District. Here they are using former Maidstone & District Leyland National OKJ508M seen in the town centre. Stagecoach acquired both Hastings & District and Top Line in December 1989. **22 July 1989**

BELOW LEFT: Former Maidstone & District MCW Bodied Leyland Atlantean 5713 has become a tree lopper and renumbered into the service vehicle fleet as P10; as evidenced by the sign on the front it was also used for towing. It is parked outside Hawkhurst garage. **22 July 1989**

BELOW RIGHT: In the previous volume OFN721F was illustrated in use as a ticket office in Hastings in 1980. Nine years later it still exists and is now owned by Maidstone & District as service vehicle P145. It is parked outside Hawkhurst garage. **22 July 1989**

ABOVE LEFT: Preserved East Kent Guy Arab III FFN382 with Park Royal bodywork similar to that carried by London's RT class is seen on display at a bus rally in Gravesend. **23 July 1989**

ABOVE RIGHT: Magnificent Maidstone & District Leyland Olympian coach 5451 was new in 1985 and carried Invictaway livery similar to the vehicle alongside outside Gillingham garage. In April 1989 it was repainted into this "Olau Line" livery which it retained until disposal in late 1990. **23 July 1989**

RIGHT: New Enterprise 54 was new as London 'DMS' Daimler Fleetline DMS1614. The smart grey and red livery is derived from the M&D style and the bus is just leaving Borough Green railway station. (compare this with the earlier photo taken on 24 Jun 88). **29 July 1989**

BELOW LEFT: Former East Kent Leyland National GFN549N sold in November 1988 has joined the fleet of "Pride of the Road" in Barnsley and is seen leaving the town bus station. **9 September 1989**

BELOW RIGHT: Grimethorpe is a well known mining town and former East Kent Leyland National EFN167L is depicted in Barnsley bus station working that service whilst in the ownership of "Pride of the Road". **9 September 1989**

LEFT: The Showbus rally was held at Woburn Abbey for many years before moving to Duxford. Maidstone & District and East Kent always provided several vehicles. Here long wheelbase Invictaway liveried Olympian, Maidstone & District 5453 new in June 1986 still looks new three years later. **24 September 1989**

BELOW: Former LT DMS2069 had been new in 1976 and was one of 20 similar vehicles acquired by Maidstone & District in 1982. It stands on the exit ramp of Chatham Pentagon bus station. It would later operate for the New Enterprise subsidiary (see Dec 91 photo later in this book) before sale in 1993 after which it operated for Green Lane Travel in North London. **30 September 1989**

BELOW LEFT: Former London DM1138 had already had a varied life before it became Maidstone & District driver trainer P001 in August 1988. After sale by LT it was operated on Round London Sightseeing Tours by Ebdon of Sidcup, it then passed to the New Enterprise fleet in 1986 for service operation. Seen here at Chatham (Luton) garage. **28 December 1989**

BELOW RIGHT: Maidstone & District had acquired some new Dennis Dominators in 1980 and the opportunity was taken to acquire suitable second hand examples. 5316 had been new to Merseyside PTE in 1980 and carries a Willowbrook body. It is about to enter Chatham Pentagon bus station with winter sun casting dark shadows. **13 January 1990**

ABOVE: Ex Maidstone & District 5123 is now 523 in the Hastings & District fleet. It is seen parked in Hastings coach station in the red/cream livery next to other examples in the standard blue/yellow livery. **3 March 1990**

RIGHT: Hastings & District purchased several second hand Bristol REs as represented here in Hastings by 423 acquired from Northern (Wigmores) in August 1989 working route 10 to Bexhill. **3 March 1990**

RIGHT: Maidstone & District Bristol VRT 5845 seen in Mount Pleasant Road Tunbridge Wells carried this overall advertisement livery for PB Aluminium from June 1988 to June 1990. 19 May 1990. **19 May 1990**

ABOVE LEFT: Leyland Leopards 3462, 3459 & 3452 parked in Edenbridge garage still had several more years life left with M&D since the large numbers of Leyland Nationals in the fleet were deemed unsuitable for the Edenbridge routes. **19 May 1990**

ABOVE RIGHT: Maidstone & District Leyland National 3549 seen parked at Hawkhurst bus station which is adjacent to the garage. Behind is a National in dual purpose livery. The white cover next to the blind display is the visible sign of the fitting of an attack alarm. **28 May 1990**

BELOW: Former East Kent AEC Reliance touring coach UFN483H is now in the fleet of Farleigh Coaches in whose Wouldham yard it was captured on film. **2 June 1990**

ABOVE: Hunt's of Alford in Lincolnshire had acquired this Park Royal bodied Atlantean OTY412M by November 1989. It had been new to Northern General and was acquired by East Kent in June 1986 as their fleet number 7412 and sold in June 1989 to Ripley Carlton. It stands in their workshop before sale again to Jones LLanerchymedd on Anglesey in October 1990. **10 June 1990**

LEFT: Former Maidstone & District Bristol VRT 5734 had been new in June 1975. It is one of four vehicles from this batch that has now been acquired by Eastern Counties for operation in Norwich. Its new fleet number is HVR334 the 'H' indicating 'High' since other ECOC VRTs were built to lower heights. This is also visibly indicated by the cream roof to make them easily identified by ECOC staff. Compare this livery with that prior to privatisation as illustrated on page 14. **21 June 1990**

45

ABOVE LEFT: Earlier in this book I illustrated two former East Kent RFN...G fleetlines in Cambridge with Guide Friday. A year later we find a third: RFN965G working the tour. **23 June 1990**

ABOVE RIGHT: IIn 1987 and 1988 Maidstone & District acquired 15 Leyland Atlanteans from Greater Manchester Buses. 5723 LJA644P carries a unibus advertisement for the Chequers shopping centre. It is parked at the Boro'line depot in Maidstone which M&D used as an outstation following closure of their own garage in Maidstone in 1981. **28 July 1990**

RIGHT: Maidstone & District suburban coach specification Leyland National 3902 stands in the Boroline depot at Maidstone. This bus would be sold for scrap the following year. **28 July 1990**

BELOW LEFT: Maidstone & District MCW Metrobus MKII 5205 carried this overall advertisement for Swale Motors for 2 ½ years. Seen here on the outskirts of Chatham. **28 July 1990**

BELOW RIGHT: In contrast to the previous photograph Swale Motors also sponsored the painting of Bristol VRT 5855 in the same livery for over 5 years. It is parked between duties in Sittingbourne garage. **28 July 1990**

ABOVE: Withdrawn stock in Sittingbourne garage includes these two Bristol VRTs and two ex London DMS class Fleetlines. C745 (KKE745N) is a rare VRT2 bodied to full height, it was renumbered from 5745 to indicate it was part of the private hire fleet. The other vehicles are VRT 5830 and ex LT DMSs 5022/5024. All four vehicles were sold to PVS for scrap in October 1990. **28 July 1990**

ABOVE LEFT: East Kent mid height Bristol VRT 7656 seen in Faversham working route 603 to Canterbury. **28 July 1990**

ABOVE RIGHT: These two former Greater Manchester buses Atlanteans joined the fleet of East Kent in December 1987. Standing at Herne Bay garage their new fleet numbers are 7503 and 7557. Behind is an ex Tyne & Wear yellow Bristol LH, one of four acquired for training duties in March 1990. 7557 was sold for scrap in August being replaced by a new Olympian. 7503 would have the honour of being the last former ex GMPTE Atlantean in service being withdrawn in December 1990. **28 July 1990**

LEFT: Brand new and yet to enter service a line of East Kent long wheelbase Leyland Olympians in store in Herne Bay garage. They carry Northern Counties bodies and 'H' registration plates that are only valid from 1 Aug 1990. Visible are 7810 and 7808. **28 July 1990**

ABOVE LEFT: New East Kent Olympian 7810 the last of the batch of 10 with Northern Counties bodywork was reversed out of Herne Bay garage to allow this photograph to be taken. **28 July 1990**

ABOVE RIGHT: Former East Kent Alexander bodied AEC Swift YJG584K has now been bought by Northbourne Park School. It is parked at Thanet (Westwood) garage. **28 July 1990**

LEFT: Withdrawn stock at Thanet (Westwood) garage includes these three Atlanteans displaced by the new Leyland Olympians pictured earlier. New to East Kent 7011 with ECW body and former Greater Manchester Buses Northern Counties bodied 7113 and 7112, these latter two had only served East Kent for three years. **28 July 1990**

BELOW LEFT: : A surprise purchase by East Kent in 1989 was a pair of Alexander bodied Scania N113DRBs, both of which still serve the company well. They were purchased from dealer stock to replace two Atlanteans destroyed by fire. The second of the two 7782 stands inside Thanet (Westwood) garage. **28 July 1990**

BELOW RIGHT: Preserved East Kent FFN399 a 1951 Guy Arab III with Park Royal body seen inside Thanet (Westwood) garage. **28 July 1990**

ABOVE LEFT: East Kent driver training bus P193 is a 1967 AEC Regent V with bodywork by Park Royal. Note the application of the new East Kent fleetname and stripes. It stands in the yard of Thanet (Westwood) garage next to a Boro'line coach being used for the club tour. **28 July 1990**

ABOVE RIGHT: Also at Thanet (Westwood) garage are other vehicles in the East Kent training fleet. Regent V MFN943F is now P195 and two Bristol LHs acquired specifically from Tyne & Wear for such work are on the left LGR647P (P187) and on the right is HJT45N (P185). **28 July 1990**

RIGHT: Former Greater Manchester Buses Leyland Atlantean with Northern Counties body HNB44N is now East Kent 7844, it poses for the camera outside Thanet (Westwood) garage. This bus would be sold for scrap in September 1990. **28 July 1990**

BELOW LEFT: This East Kent Bristol VRT 7682 carries an all over advertisement for Coastways local dealers for Citroen cars seen at Thanet (Westwood) garage. **28 July 1990**

BELOW RIGHT: In 1982 East Kent received eleven Leyland Leopards with ECW 'B51' bodies for National Express work. The livery of white with black skirt and bumpers did nothing to improve the styling of these coaches. 8831 stands in the doorway of Thanet (Westwood) garage. **28 July 1990**

ABOVE LEFT: G&S Travel parked vehicles at the premises of Thanet Commercials as represented here by semi-preserved former Maidstone & District Leyland Atlantean 597UKM. **28 July 1990**

BELOW LEFT: East Kent MCW Metrobus II fleet number 7750 loads up in Canterbury bus station in preparation for its trip to Broadstairs. **28 July 1990**

ABOVE RIGHT: East Kent 1083 is a Leyland National built to Suburban coach specification. Here it is parked in Canterbury bus station with blinds for the Park and Ride service. **28 July 1990**

BELOW RIGHT: East Kent Bristol VRT 7656 stands in Canterbury bus station, the livery certainly suits the vehicle very well. **28 July 1990**

BELOW: In comparison to the livery worn by 8831 seen on the previous page the East Kent Coaches livery on this similar vehicle 8835 is a marked improvement. It is seen here in Canterbury bus station outside the travel office which also carries the new East Kent colour scheme and has since been demolished. **28 July 1990**

ABOVE: Approaching Hempstead Valley Shopping Centre is Maidstone & District 5905 the last of a batch of five Leyland Olympians delivered new in April 1990. Fleet livery with M&D logos either side of the blind display limited frontal advertising to the small space under the windscreen. **11 August 1990**

RIGHT: Maidstone & District Dennis Dominator 5311 had been new to East Staffordshire District Council in May 1979 and was one of nine similar vehicles acquired in 1985. It carries an East Lancs body with its distinctive peaked front dome. It is arriving at Hempstead Valley Shopping Centre on a sunny summer day. **11 August 1990**

RIGHT: Compare this Dennis Dominator with Willowbrook body with the previous photograph taken in the same place. Maidstone & District 5304 was new in 1980. **11 August 1990**

ABOVE LEFT: Maidstone & District minibus 1054 emerges from the Pentagon bus station carrying an all over advertisement livery for Skipaway. **1 September 1990**
ABOVE RIGHT: Maidstone & District operated the open top Rochester tour in 1990 using this Leyland Atlantean 5706 seen here in Chatham. Note the fixed destination details.
1 September 1990

ABOVE: Maidstone & District 5316 is a Willowbrook bodied Dennis Dominator acquired from Merseyside PTE in December 1986. Note the fitting of an electronic destination display as it leaves Chatham Pentagon bus station.
1 September 1990

BELOW: Kent Constabulary acquired this former East Kent Atlantean HNB45N which had been new to Greater Manchester Buses. It is seen on display at a typically wet Showbus rally at Woburn Abbey. **30 September 1990**

ABOVE: Maidstone & District 5266 was the first of five Metrobuses delivered in 1980 for NBC comparison trials between Metrobuses, Dennis Dominators and Bristol VRTs. Originally five Leyland Titans had also been due before the order was cancelled and they ended up elsewhere. Seen here devoid of advertisements following repaint it is on the entrance ramp to Chatham Pentagon bus station. This bus would later be transferred to the New Enterprise fleet in 1993 for further service. **1 September 1990**

BELOW: East Kent Northern Counties bodied Leyland Olympians 7807 from Herne Bay garage and 7806 from Ashford garage are just a couple of months old and are on display at the Showbus rally at Woburn Abbey. All five Herne Bay based Olympians were named following a Children's competition. 7807 has been named 'Enterprise' and won first prize in Class 14 (post 1980 double deckers in service). **30 September 1990**

ABOVE LEFT: Maidstone & District Leyland Tiger / Duple 340 style bodywork 2189 on a club trip to South Wales and Bristol stands in Newport bus station, this trip stands in the memory as one of the wettest day trips undertaken by the club with almost constant rain. **6 April 1991**

ABOVE RIGHT: Hasting & District former East Kent AEC Regent V MFN946F seen on display at Addlestone during the annual Cobham bus museum open day and bus gathering. **7 April 1991**

LEFT: Numerically the first ex London Transport DMS Fleetline in Maidstone & District stock is 5021 the former DMS 1658 seen here at Hempstead Valley shopping centre, this bus would later work for New Enterprise and is pictured as such later in this book. **11 May 1991**

LEFT: This DMS is in the new Maidstone & District livery with additional cream 5037 was formerly DMS1955 seen awaiting departure from Hempstead Valley shopping centre. This bus still exists with the Gravesham Crime Prevention panel and is regularly used during the summer months. **11 May 1991**

ABOVE LEFT: Two New Enterprise coaches in their Tonbridge yard on the left is No.14 AKP430T a Plaxton bodied Bedford YMT acquired from Sonner of Gillingham in 1981. On the right is No.23 TSU645 which was previously Maidstone & District 2645 and originally registered FKL173L, it is a Plaxton bodied Leyland Tiger and was acquired in December 1990. **11 May 1991**

ABOVE RIGHT: Maidstone & District acquired this Mercedes-Benz L508D/Whittaker C19F from Biss of Bishops Stortford in 1988 for use as a minibus trainer. UEV249W stands in the corner of Tunbridge Wells garage. **18 May 1991**

BELOW: This series 2 Bristol VRT was originally Maidstone & District 5827, in this view is it now owned by Warrens of Ticehurst and is passing their garage. **18 May 1991**

BELOW LEFT: Wearing green and cream livery of Maidstone & District is this 1977 Leyland National numbered 3555 seen parked inside Tunbridge Wells garage. **18 May 1991**

BELOW RIGHT: This is East Kent 8843 their first MCW Metroliner coach now re-registered to 6540FN from FKK843Y. The East Kent coaching livery suits the vehicle well. On hire to the Maidstone & District and East Kent Bus Club for a day trip it is seen in the Boro'line yard at Crayford from where they operated their London based operations. **18 May 1991**

ABOVE LEFT: Two preserved vehicles on display at the Southend bus rally. East Kent AEC Regent V PFN874 new in 1959 stands next to Maidstone & District Leyland Atlantean 5558 new in 1960. **2 June 1991**

ABOVE RIGHT: A club trip to Banbury finds this former East Kent AEC Regent V GJD747D now owned by the St. John Ambulance Banbury Marching Band. **29 June 1991**

LEFT: Hastings & District sold their pair of AEC Regals to Guide Friday for further use on Sightseeing tours in November 1989. Here HKL826 new in 1946 is seen in Upper Slaughter while operating the Cotswold Tour. It has been forced to a stop since the coach hired by the club for this trip was blocking its route. The tourists were somewhat surprised to be the centre of attention for numerous cameras! **29 June 1991**

BELOW LEFT: The Bexley Show finds former Maidstone & District Leyland Atlantean 5718 in use by the H.E. Services JCB Stunt Team. **13 July 1991**

BELOW RIGHT: Maidstone & District Service vehicle P99 was former 5739 and used as a mobile advertisement hoarding. On display here at the Bexley Show. It was actually owned by M&D Advertising Ltd. **13 July 1991**

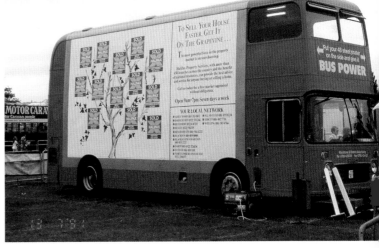

ABOVE LEFT: East Kent acquired this former London Country Leyland National in 1984 for use on shuttle services to Dover docks. NPD156L carries the livery for Sealink and has had its seating capacity reduced from 49 to 30 to allow more standing passengers and luggage space. **20 July 1991**

ABOVE RIGHT: East Kent branded their minibuses as EK Minilink as witnessed here by 664 a Freight Rover Sherpa one of several acquired from Eastern Counties in 1989 in exchange for Ford Transits in the interests of standardisation in both fleets. It stands in Dover. **20 July 1991**

LEFT: Fuggles of Benenden GKK160V was new to Maidstone & District as 2160, but was acquired from New Enterprise. It is a Leyland Leopard with Willowbrook DP49F body. It displays its smart livery in Holywell Avenue Folkestone. **20 July 1991**

BELOW LEFT: East Kent Expressliner 8904 is a Volvo B10M with Plaxton Paramount 3500 3 body. Seen here calling in Hythe. **20 July 1991**

BELOW RIGHT: East Kent highbridge Bristol VRT 7043 also seen in Hythe on route to Folkestone. **20 July 1991**

ABOVE LEFT: This Leyland National 2 CPO100W had been new to City of Portsmouth, it has reached Hastings via Southdown. Now numbered 142 in the Stagecoach South Coast Buses fleet it is seen in Hastings and is now preserved. **20 July 1991**

ABOVE RIGHT: Stagecoach South Coast Buses minibus 2849 is parked in the corner of the yard at Silverhill (Hastings) garage. **20 July 1991**

BELOW LEFT: Another Leyland National 2 that has reached Hastings from Portsmouth is ERV115W now numbered 143 in the Stagecoach South Coast Buses fleet. It stands in the yard at Silverhill (Hastings) garage. **20 July 1991**

BELOW RIGHT: Stagecoach South Coast Buses 1185 is a Duple/Hestair. It now carries a registration plate 420DCD from a Southdown 'Queen Mary' and is being inspected by club members inside Silverhill (Hastings) garage. **20 July 1991**

LEFT: Seen in Hythe is East Kent Mk 2 Metrobus 7762 one of the batch of seven fitted with high back seating. **20 July 1991**

LEFT: A consequence of the purchase of Hastings & District by Stagecoach is the transfer in of many vehicles that originated with Southdown. Here new Southdown Leyland National YCD74T shows its Hastings buses fleetname at Silverhill (Hastings) garage. **20 July 1991**

LEFT: Eastbourne Buses acquired several of these former East Kent ECW bodied Leyland Atlanteans. Here JJG6P loads up in Eastbourne as their fleet number 33. **20 July 1991**

LEFT: Similar vehicle Eastbourne Buses 32 new to East Kent, JJG2P passes Eastbourne railway station. Note the livery variation compared to the previous photograph. **20 July 1991**

ABOVE LEFT: This Leyland Tiger with Plaxton DP53F body had been new to London Country as TP14, but was acquired by Maidstone & District from London Buses Ltd. As acquired it was registered A114EPA, but was registered YSU895 in December 1990. Its M&D fleet number was 2172. It is awaiting attention at Hawkhurst garage. **20 July 1991**

ABOVE RIGHT: Maidstone & District service vehicle P55 is a Bedford KDL lorry fitted with a crane. It was new in January 1976 and finally sold in March 1995 and spent its life at Hawkhurst garage where it is seen here. **20 July 1991**

LEFT: Late in the evening in the yard of Fuggles of Benenden stand this pair of former Maidstone & District dual purpose seated Leyland Nationals SKN911R and SKN910R, both of which came via Hastings and District **20 July 1991**

BELOW: The vehicle that started the Big Bus Sightseeing Tour and whose outline is used in their marketing logo. Former East Kent AEC Regent V PFN853 is loading up at Marble Arch. **28 July 1991**

ABOVE: Former East Kent AEC Regent V PFN853 is a magnificent sight as it rounds Marble Arch on the Big Bus Sightseeing Tour. The Big Bus livery is very similar to that it carried with East Kent. **28 July 1991**

LEFT: This was Maidstone & District SO43 and was new in 1950. It is a Bristol L6A with bodywork by ECW. Now preserved it is on display at the Sevenoaks rally. This was a late example of Bristol/ECW production for a non Tilling company after 1948 having been ordered before the 'shutters' came down'. Former Maidstone & District 25 TKR is visible behind. **4 August 1991**

BELOW: Folkestone bus station finds East Kent Bristol VRT 7657 new in 1980 alongside Leyland National 1552 new in 1975 and now used on Sealink services. **7 September 1991**

LEFT: 1991 was the 75th anniversary of East Kent and to celebrate a rally was held at the Eurotunnel exhibition site. In attendance was preserved MFN888 a 1956 Guy Arab with Park Royal body. **7 September 1991**

BELOW: New East Kent DAF Delta 1401 bought for the Canterbury Park & Ride service was licensed for service on 1 September, it is seen before entry into service at the East Kent 75th anniversary rally at the Eurotunnel exhibition site. The three Deltas for this service were the first new full size single deckers in the East Kent fleet for fourteen years. **7 September 1991**

BOTTOM: Liberally adorned with front advertising East Kent Leyland Olympian 7803 stands in Folkestone bus station. **7 September 1991**

ABOVE: Coach seated East Kent Mk 2 Metrobus 7761 is the first of the batch and was new in spring 1989 seen in Folkestone bus station on the day of the East Kent 75th anniversary rally. Note the '75 years' logos on the side panels. **7 September 1991**

LEFT: The East Kent Minilink sticker in the front windscreen is the only outward sign that this Iveco minibus has been acquired from Brighton & Hove by East Kent and numbered 230 in the East Kent fleet. It was acquired in June 1990 and is parked in Folkestone bus station. It was painted white for the application of an overall advertisement which fell through. **7 September 1991**

LEFT: Former East Kent AEC Regent V PFN852 was pictured on the back cover of the previous book as a driver trainer with Derby City Transport in 1985. Six years later it retains the same livery, but has moved to Luton & District and is on display at the Woburn Showbus rally. **29 September 1991**

ABOVE: The Showbus rally at Woburn and we find East Kent Metrobus 7755 repainted into traditional livery for the 75th anniversary of East Kent, note the side advertisement banner explaining the event. Behind is Leyland Olympian 7807. **29 September 1991**

RIGHT: This 1945 Bristol K6A was rebodied by Weymann in 1953. It is owned by members of the M&D and East Kent Bus Club and is seen here at Mote Park Maidstone during their AGM. **30 November 1991**

RIGHT: Still owned by the company at this time this 1951 Commer Avenger with Harrington C16F body was an executive coach used by the Directors of Maidstone & District. It was named "The Knightrider"; the company's head office being situated in Knightrider House Maidstone. Seen at Mote Park Maidstone. **30 November 1991**

LEFT: Between November and February seven Wilts & Dorset DMS Fleetlines were loaned to Maidstone & District. Two of these were used by New Enterprise during December. Here DMS2231 with temporary fleet number 5046 stand in the Tonbridge yard of New Enterprise. **7 December 1991**

LEFT: In contrast to the previous photograph here is one of Maidstone & District's own DMSs. DMS2106 is now M&D 5032 seen in Maidstone underneath the Christmas lights. **14 December 1991**

LEFT: Maidstone & District 5036 originally DM1952 has now become P38 in the service vehicle fleet. It was a towing vehicle, but also contained a water tank upstairs to allow the ceiling lights in the Pentagon bus station to be cleaned. Seen here parked in Hart Street Maidstone this being a temporary base for the Maidstone based fleet. **14 December 1991**

ABOVE: Maidstone & District acquired the Tunbridge Wells based stage operation of Shearings Ltd and with it four Leyland Lynx on 2 December 1991. This is 3048 which has still to gain Maidstone & District fleetnames or livery. It is standing at Chatham. **21 December 1991**

CENTRE RIGHT: By mid 1991 the New Enterprise DMS stock had reduced to the two vehicles seen here in the Tonbridge yard. Notice the livery variation, on the left is No.55 which was transferred from the main Maidstone & District fleet in October 1990 and next to it is No. 54 which came with the company in 1988. The appearance of No. 54 is considerably enhanced from that shown earlier in this book (on 24 Jun 88). **29 December 1991**

RIGHT: The potential sale of Boroline Maidstone posed a commercial threat to the Maidstone & District business. As a result M&D withdrew their operations from the Boroline garage in Armstrong Road and set up new commercial services in Maidstone together with a new yard in Hart Street. Additional vehicles were required and thus between November 1991 and February 1992 seven DMS class Daimler Fleetlines from Wilts & Dorset were hired, a type already well known to M&D. Two of these seven also operated for a short period with New Enterprise. However they were not popular with drivers since unlike the M&D examples they lacked cab heaters. DMS2045 seen here in Chatham was given temporary fleet number 5041. **30 December 1991**

LEFT: For three years Maidstone & District Bristol VRT 5847 carried this overall advertisement for Safeway food stores, it is seen at Chatham railway station. **30 December 1991**

LEFT: The original 5025 was DM1737 which was written off after an accident in August 1988. Its replacement was DM1830 seen here leaving Chatham station which came from the New Enterprise fleet. Unusually the reflective front number plate on this bus has been mounted on the indentation for the front air intakes. **30 December 1991**

BELOW: A selection of types seen in the rear yard of Chatham (Luton) garage. DMS2225 with DMS2193 behind are on hire from Wilts & Dorset and carry temporary fleet numbers 5045 and 5044 respectively. 5045 is just visible on the front centre white band. Also visible is Northern Counties bodied Leyland Olympian 5901 and Willowbrook bodied Dennis Dominator 5305. **30 December 1991**

ABOVE: Sharing the rear yard of Chatham (Luton) bus station are ex LT DMSs 1947 and 1958 now numbered 5035 and 5039 with Maidstone & District. Parked beyond these is an ex East Staffordshire East Lancs bodied Dennis Dominator 5315 (PRE39W). **30 December 1991**

RIGHT: The front yard of Maidstone & District Chatham (Luton) garage and we see ex LT DMS2190 on hire from Wilts & Dorset with temporary fleet number 5042. **30 December 1991**

RIGHT: Just six weeks old and part of the first Maidstone & District order for Dennis Darts 3465 swings into Gillingham bus station en route to Sittingbourne. **30 December 1991**

ABOVE LEFT: On route 101 between Maidstone and Chatham former LT DMS 2045 is currently on hire to Maidstone & District from Wilts & Dorset with temporary fleet number 5041. In the late December gloom it stands at Gillingham bus station. **30 December 1991**

ABOVE RIGHT: A sad end is nigh for former Maidstone & District coach 4610 a 1968 Leyland Leopard with Duple Commander III body seen here 'abandoned' in a field just south of Ipswich. **4 April 1992**

CENTRE RIGHT: Earlier in this book (May 1989) I illustrated former East Kent AEC Regent V GJG750D with New Enterprise. Here it is again as a private hire and training vehicle with Leaside Buses. Numbered RV1 it was affectionately known as Arvie (Harvey) and was bought in May 1991 after operation by several other Kent operators. It has returned to Kent to undertake a tour for the club and is seen in Maidstone. In Spring 2006 the bus was sold to preservationists by the dealer Ensignbus. **13 June 1992**

RIGHT: Bygone buses of Biddenden are operating former Maidstone & District Bristol VRT 5826 as evidenced in this Maidstone view. **13 June 1992**

ABOVE LEFT: HNB45N had been new to Greater Manchester PTE in 1987 and was acquired by East Kent in 1987 as their 7845. On withdrawal from service it has been converted into a publicity bus for the Kent Constabulary and is seen here parked in the lower shed of Ashford garage alongside the remains of Willowbrook Bristol VRT 7984 which had been withdrawn in September 1991 following roof damage. 13 June 1992

ABOVE RIGHT: A very uninspiring livery is carried by East Kent ECW bodied Leyland Leopard 8828 in the lower shed of Ashford garage. This coach has received bus seats from TFN984T shown in the previous photo and is thus now classified as B47F. **13 June 1992**

CENTRE LEFT: The high backed coach seats can be clearly seen in this view of East Kent dual purpose Mk2 Metrobus 7762 seen outside Ashford garage. **13 June 1992**

LEFT: Highlighting the SeaCat service operated by Hoverspeed between Folkestone & Boulogne is East Kent Leyland National 1552 which works on a shuttle service, it was new in 1975 and is seen here at Folkestone bus station. **13 June 1992**

RIGHT: The revised Iveco minibus is pictured here at Dover Pencester Road. 18 was new in December 1991 whereas 94 was delivered in February 1990. **13 June 1992**

BELOW: Now preserved, but carrying the livery of its previous owner Carlton PSV of Gillingham East Kent AEC Regent V 6801FN has come to rendezvous with a club trip at Canterbury bus station. The new East Kent logo is visible on the side of the booking office behind the bus and makes an interesting contrast with that on the bus. **13 June 1992**

LEFT: East Kent minibus 13 seen in Canterbury carrying an all over advertisement for Lenleys a home furnishing store. Note the East Kent logo in the blind display there being nothing else to identify its owner. **13 June 1992**

LEFT: East Kent Metroliner coach 8245 was new to Premier Travel as B245JVA and received this 'dateless' registration earlier in 1992. It is seen in the coach park in Barnstaple, Devon. **8 October 1992**

CENTRE LEFT: New to East Kent as 1178 this Leyland National is now in the fleet of Kinch in whose yard at Barrow upon Soar it was captured on film. Happily this bus is now preserved and back in East Kent livery **14 October 1992**

CENTRE RIGHT: This little Dennis Falcon P3 with Dennis B25F body was built in 1950 as a twenty seater, but was converted in 1956 when it was adapted for one person operation. Withdrawn in 1967 it first entered preservation in 1970 and downseated again. It is seen here at Mote Park Maidstone during an AGM of the M&D and East Kent Bus club. **28 November 1992**

LEFT: This 1971 Leyland Atlantean with ECW body JJG1P has retained East Kent livery with its new owner Kingsley's of Birtley, Tyne & Wear at whose premises it is pictured. **5 April 1993**

71

LEFT: A second former East Kent ECW bodied Leyland Atlantean in the Kingsley's fleet is JJG9P seen in the road outside their garage in Portobello, Birtley. **5 April 1993**

CENTRE LEFT: The bus shelter tells us that this is the Queens Monument stop in Maidstone. Maidstone & District Leyland Atlantean 'special' 5708 was destined to be the very last of this batch in use a couple of years after this photograph was taken, it is about to depart for Snodland. **17 April 1993**

BELOW LEFT: The different heights of these two East Kent Bristol VRTs in Folkestone bus station is evident. Mid height 7665 stands next to full height 7043. **5 June 1993**

BELOW RIGHT: The first 'Expressliners' were built with Plaxton Paramount 3500 3 bodies and East Kent had nine of these. A requirement for a tenth vehicle in 1993 saw delivery of this Plaxton Premiere 350 which unlike the previous vehicles had a blue side stripe at wheel level. It is parked in Pencester Road Dover. **5 June 1993**

ABOVE LEFT: Compare this Paramount bodied 'Expressliner' with the Premier example pictured on the previous page in the same spot, Pencester Road Dover. East Kent 8901 was the first of the batch delivered new in September 1989. **5 June 1993**

ABOVE RIGHT: It is interesting to compare this view of ex LCBS LNB67 with that earlier in this book (on 16 Aug 86). Previously numbered 1067 in the East Kent fleet it is now 1167, other changes apart from livery affect the blind display. The earlier livery reflects the British ownership of Sealink whereas this view cites Stena Sealink, Stena is based in Sweden and claims to be 'The world's leading Ferry Company'. It is pictured outside Dover garage. **5 June 1993**

CENTRE RIGHT: Mercury Passenger Services based in Hoo Kent were operating this former East Kent ECW bodied Leyland Atlantean JJG5P at the time of my visit. **13 June 1993**

RIGHT: Folkestone bus station is the setting for this view of full height East Kent Bristol VRT 7042, New in 1976 it has already notched up 17 years service for the company. **19 June 1993**

RIGHT: Delivered the previous month East Kent Leyland Olympian 7824 was based at Herne Bay garage being the nearest garage to Canterbury. It awaits its next journey in Canterbury bus station. **19 June 1993**

BELOW : Herne Bay High Street is the setting for these two East Kent Willowbrook bodied Bristol VRTs 7990 leads 7023. **19 June 1993**

BELOW RIGHT: Earlier in this book (on 6 Aug 88) I illustrated 8399 as acquired from MCW. It has now been re-registered again to become XDU599. It is almost 10 years old, but still looks modern as it is about to depart from Herne Bay garage. **3 July 1993**

RIGHT: A pair of Willowbrook bodied Bristol VRTs in Herne Bay garage yard, 7985 is behind 7987. **3 July 1993**

ABOVE LEFT: Dual purpose East Kent Leyland National 1184 in all over advertisement livery for Sainsbury's in the yard at Herne Bay garage. **3 July 1993**

ABOVE RIGHT: Originally registered FKK842Y when new in 1983 this East Kent Paramount bodied Leyland Tiger with fleet number 8842 stands inside Thanet (Westwood) garage. **3 July 1993**

BELOW LEFT: Sole survivor of the batch of twelve Alexander bodied AEC Swifts which will forever be associated with Dover garage is YJG587K which although still carries its service fleet number (1587) on the front panel is now P197 in the service vehicle fleet and was retained for use as a tow bus at Thanet (Westwood) garage where it is pictured. **3 July 1993**

BELOW RIGHT: East Kent 8996 a Bova Futura acquired with the business of Marinair has swopped its original registration of C996FKM for PFN873 which came from the AEC Regent V carnival bus pictured earlier in this book. It is seen at Thanet (Westwood) garage. **3 July 1993**

LEFT: This 1928 Hastings Tramways Guy BTX trolleybus DY4965 is a familiar sight to those living on the south east coast. It was transferred to Maidstone & District in 1957 and fitted with a Commer TS3 diesel engine in 1960 so that it could continue in use at special events and carnivals. It is now in the care of Hastings Borough Council and is seen here with a full load at a bus rally in Eastbourne. **18 July 1993**

RIGHT: Compare this view of newly restored preserved Maidstone & District Leyland Panther with that shown earlier (16 May 87). LKT132F is on display at a bus rally on Eastbourne sea front. **18 July 1993**

BELOW LEFT: Gillingham garage is the location of this shot of Maidstone & District Leyland Atlantean 'special'. 5706 was converted to open top in Spring 1988, note the high standard of presentation even down to the wording on the tyres. **24 July 1993**

BELOW RIGHT: Maidstone & District long wheelbase Olympian 5445 is now ten years old and to disguise this fact had been re-registered to YSU867 in October 1990. The paintwork gleams in this view inside Gillingham garage. **24 July 1993**

BOTTOM: Numerically the last Bristol VRT delivered to Maidstone & District *and* used in service was this bus 5886 (5887 & 5888 were the first two of a subsequent order which arrived before that order was cancelled and they were transferred to Thames Valley and Aldershot without being used). It is pictured on route 101 in Gillingham bus station. **24 July 1993**

LEFT: Restored and preserved by the company is this 1960 Leyland Atlantean 5558. it carries Metro-Cammell H44/33F bodywork and has advertising for the company history. Specifically posed for photographs at Gillingham garage. Happily this bus survives in 2006 with Chatham Historic Dockyard. **24 July 1993**

ABOVE LEFT: Maidstone & District 2170 a Leyland Leopard coach with ECW DP49F body seen at Gillingham garage in Invictaway livery. **24 July 1993**

ABOVE RIGHT: Maidstone & District's Gillingham garage finds these two re-registered Leyland Tigers with Duple Dominant II Express bodies. Delivered new to M&D in 1980 as JKK161V and JKK163V and numbered 2161 & 2163 they would remain in the fleet until sold in 1995. **24 July 1993**

BELOW LEFT: Magnificent 1937 Leyland TS8 with Park Royal C32R body JG9938 had survived with East Kent as a mobile office. It was sold to Smith of Sittingbourne in July 1988 who carried out extensive restoration over several years and painted it in his livery. It is seen here in his yard ready for use by members of the M&D and East Kent Bus Club on a local tour. **24 July 1993**

BELOW RIGHT: Maidstone Queens Monument is the setting for Maidstone & District Leyland Olympian 5900 with distinctive body by Northern Counties working on a Park & Ride service. **24 July 1993**

RIGHT: On the other side of the road in Maidstone town centre we find Maidstone & District Leyland Olympian 5907 that was new in January 1993. East Kent Willowbrook bodied Bristol VRT 7974 is about to overtake. **24 July 1993**

CENTRE RIGHT: New for Invictaway services in 1983 Maidstone & District long wheelbase Leyland Olympian 5442 has been cascaded down to dual purpose livery and used on some of the longer 'local' services such as route 5 from Maidstone to Hastings as shown here at Maidstone Queens Monument. **24 July 1993**

LEFT: A rare treat for members of the M&D and East Kent bus club was a visit to Iden Grange, Staplehurst. Seen there is East Kent CJG959 a 1947 Leyland Titan PD1A with Leyland L27/26R body owned by members of the club, alongside is Maidstone & District FKL611 which carries a Weymann body built in 1936 and originally fitted to a Bristol GO5G chassis, but this was found unsuitable and it was re-fitted to this new K5G chassis in 1938. **24 July 1993**

LEFT: In 1976 Maidstone & District received a batch of 7 Bristol VRTs with the Leyland 501 engine. Four of these were transferred to Hastings and District in 1983. Two others were scrapped in 1991 and this left 5120 as the sole survivor, seen here at picturesque Tenterden on route 12. **24 July 1993.**

CENTRE LEFT: Numbered OR1 in the Maidstone & District fleet HKL819 was the only one of the three so converted not transferred to Hastings & District and this 1946 AEC Regal has since passed into preservation. It is seen here on display at the Sevenoaks bus rally repainted back into M&D livery. **8 August 1993**

BELOW LEFT: Motts garage at Stoke Mandeville is the location for this former East Kent Leyland Leopard 8830 it is now Motts No.8. **15 August 1993**

BELOW RIGHT: Kinch's former East Kent Leyland National EFN178L is captured on film passing the Broad Marsh Shopping Centre en route to the Clifton suburb of Nottingham. **3 September 1993**

RIGHT: This 1962 AEC Reliance was delivered new to Maidstone & District as S325 (325NKT). In 1974 it was converted to open top as illustrated in the previous volume. M&D sold it for scrap in July 1978, but it was saved and passed through several owners losing its original registration (325NKT) in March 1990 before reaching London & Country in February 1993 pictured here in the rain at Cranleigh garage. **2 October 1993**

LEFT: Delivered for NBC comparison trials in 1980 between the Metrobus, Bristol VRT and Dennis Dominator Maidstone & District Dennis Dominator 5301 is parked on the exit ramp of Chatham Pentagon bus station. **2 April 1994**

LEFT: A double deck Rover ! Maidstone & District 5728 a former Greater Manchester buses Leyland Atlantean received this innovative all over advertisement in February 1994 for Dutton-Forshaw motor dealers. It is seen at work at Maidstone Queens Monument. **2 April 1994**

LEFT: Seen in service in Tunbridge Wells is Volvo's answer to the Dennis Dart Maidstone & District 3610 the last of a batch of ten Volvo B6s with Plaxton Pointer B40F+17 bodies delivered in March and April to Tunbridge Wells garage. The Volvo badge on the lower front panel can be seen. **14 May 1994**

RIGHT: In June 1993 six Leyland Leopards were purchased from Western Scottish to update the Edenbridge fleet. Here 3006 YCS92T is en route to Tonbridge at Chiddingstone Causeway on service 210. **14 May 1994**

RIGHT: The first of the 1981 batch of ECW bodied Bristol VRTs for East Kent 7676 stands on the forecourt of Ashford garage. **25 June 1994**

RIGHT: In order to alleviate capacity problems on the Canterbury Park and Ride service East Kent repainted Olympian 7801 for use on this service in November 1993. It stands in Canterbury; note the reverse writing on the lower front panel to get the message across to motorists using their rear view mirror. **25 June 1994**

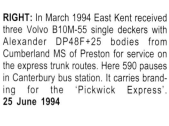

RIGHT: In March 1994 East Kent received three Volvo B10M-55 single deckers with Alexander DP48F+25 bodies from Cumberland MS of Preston for service on the express trunk routes. Here 590 pauses in Canterbury bus station. It carries branding for the 'Pickwick Express'. **25 June 1994**

RIGHT: Canterbury bus station and East Kent Mk 2 Metrobus 7749 waits between duties. Note the alteration of the legal lettering following the takeover by Stagecoach. **25 June 1994**

LEFT: Apart from dedicated Olympian 7801 other double deckers were used on the Canterbury Park and Ride service at peak times. Willowbrook Bristol VRT 7990 departs from Canterbury. **25 June 1994**

LEFT: In 1989 East Kent received two Scania N113DRBs with Alexander bodies. Initially allocated to Thanet they have now moved to Herne Bay as evidenced here by 7781. **25 June 1994**

LEFT: Autotechs of Canterbury arranged for this East Kent Bristol VRT 7684 to carry their all over advertisement livery. It stands inside Ashford garage. **16 July 1994**

ABOVE: On hire for a Club day trip this is Maidstone & District 2195 a Leyland Tiger with Plaxton 321 body (based on a Duple design adapted when Plaxton bought out Duple). Seen at Charing this coach was new to Bebb of Llantwit Fardre in 1992 and was acquired by M&D in November 1993. **16 July 1994**

RIGHT: East Kent 7679 crosses the railway at Chartham just outside Canterbury. This ECW bodied Bristol VRT was delivered thirteen years earlier in 1981, but the crisp livery style belies that fact. **16 July 1994**

RIGHT: : It is almost one year since Stagecoach bought East Kent, but the corporate livery was still a rarity at this time. Although only one year old and thus a surprise repainting Leyland Olympian 7821 has succumbed in this Canterbury bus station view. **16 July 1994**

ABOVE: In addition to the three ex Cumberland Volvo B10M single deckers one of which was shown earlier East Kent received three new examples in June 1994. Here a month later 634 still devoid of fleet names loads in Canterbury bus station. **16 July 1994**

LEFT: Preserved East Kent AEC Regent V PFN874 shares its Broad Oak home with Guy MFN888 an ex LT Breakdown tender. **16 July 1994**

LEFT: East Kent privately owned preserved vehicles at their home base, Broad Oak. 1956 Guy Arab IV MFN888 is receiving attention alongside 1959 AEC Regent V PFN867. Just visible on the right is MFN947F which had been converted for tree-lopping (the last such instance in the fleet) and is also now preserved. **16 July 1994**

RIGHT: Withdrawn for disposal with fleetnames and legal lettering removed East Kent Bristol VRT MFN41R has served the company for 18 years. It would be handed over to Kent County Constabulary on 16 Nov 94. **16 July 1994**

RIGHT: Compare this view of East Kent 8842 with that shown a year earlier (3 July 93) and the livery change is apparent. It is a 1983 Leyland tiger with Plaxton Paramount 3200 Express body and is pictured inside Thanet (Westwood) garage. **16 July 1994**

RIGHT: East Kent Bova 8996 is the only non Expressliner coach dedicated to National Express work by the Company although eight years old it still looks modern inside Thanet (Westwood) garage. **16 July 1994**

RIGHT: New to Greater Manchester PTE this bus became East Kent 7178 when it was acquired in 1987. It is a Northern Counties bodied Leyland Atlantean and is now parked inside Thanet (Westwood) garage owned by Canterbury & Thanet Health Authority in its new role as health promotion bus. **16 July 1994**

RIGHT: 'Thomas Becket' is East Kent Olympian 7810 seen here at Thanet (Westwood) garage. The bus was one of the Herne Bay Olympians named when new in August 1990. **16 July 1994**

RIGHT: East Kent Mk 2 Metrobus 7747 now sports Stagecoach corporate livery seen also inside Thanet (Westwood) garage. **16 July 1994**

LEFT: In order to retain an open top capability East Kent purchased three convertible Bristol VRTs from Southdown in 1991 represented here by 7616 which had been new in January 1978 seen inside Thanet (Westwood) garage. **16 July 1994**

LEFT: Coach seated dual purpose East Kent Mk 2 Metrobus 7761 in Folkestone bus station on service 12 to Lydd wearing new Stagecoach livery. **16 July 1994**

LEFT: Also in Folkestone bus station working service 90 to Deal via Dover is East Kent Olympian 7828 one of a batch of 5 ordered before the Stagecoach take-over, but delivered in their colours. **16 July 1994**

ABOVE: Only one year separates these two coaches in the East Kent fleet, but the contrasting styling is stark. Metroliner 8850 (new as B850TKL in August 1984) alongside Tiger / Plaxton 8838 (new as FKK838Y in May 1983), they stand in the Folkestone garage yard. **16 July 1994**

RIGHT: Earlier in this book (April 1993) I illustrated former East Kent ECW bodied Leyland Atlantean JJG9P with Kingsley in a largely white livery. Just over one year later it is seen at their Portobello premises in a mainly dark red colour scheme. Alongside is ex LT DM970 which had once operated for Black Horse Buses in Gravesend and had reached Kingsley's via Hunt of Alford Lincolnshire. **23 October 1994**

RIGHT: Following on from the three DAF Deltas bought for the Canterbury Park and Ride in 1991 the next new vehicles were five low floor Dennis Lances SLF with unusual Berkhof bodies as seen here represented by 1404 new the previous September arriving opposite Canterbury bus station. **18 February 1995**

ABOVE LEFT: From the first batch of Plaxton Pointer Dennis Darts purchased by Maidstone & District in 1991/2 3468 is seen at the Hawkhurst bus station which adjoins the garage. **25 March 1995**

ABOVE RIGHT: In January 1995 Maidstone & District painted this Marshall bodied Leyland Leopard into traditional livery. 3456 is seen at Tunbridge Wells garage just prior to being transferred to the preserved fleet. **1 July 1995**

LEFT: This Bristol VRT was 5139 in the Maidstone & District fleet and was acquired by New Enterprise in November 1994 as their No. 59. Around this time a new brighter livery for the fleet was being considered with various shades of blue applied to a cream background. This bus was the only double decker to receive the blue/cream paint scheme in April 1995. It is seen here looking extremely smart in Tunbridge Wells High Street. **1 July 1995**

LEFT: The Edenbridge routes were maintained by six ex Western Scottish Alexander bodied Leyland Leopards as represented here by 3003 in Tunbridge Wells. **1 July 1995**

LEFT: Earlier in this book (April 1994) I illustrated 5728 in an all over advertisement livery for Dutton-Forshaw. This is the next numbered Leyland Atlantean 5729 seen in Maidstone with advertising for the same sponsor although its paint scheme is not quite so innovative as that on the previous bus. **7 October 1995**

BELOW: The latest delivery of Plaxton Pointer bodied Volvo B6s included three examples for the Maidstone Park & Ride scheme. 3612 was new in December 1994 and is seen here in Maidstone town centre. **7 October 1995**

LEFT: Maidstone & District Leyland Olympian 5891 was given this all over advertisement livery to highlight the Maidstone Town centre management initiative. It is seen loading at the Queens Monument Maidstone. **7 October 1995**

LEFT: Maidstone & District 2189 is a Duple 340 bodied Leyland Tiger used on the 'Green Line' Maidstone to London commuter express service. It stands at the rear of Maidstone garage. **2 December 1995**

LEFT: Maidstone & District 2195 is a Plaxton 321 bodied Leyland Tiger also used on the commuter service between London and Maidstone. Seen at its home garage and comparison with the previous photo shows that Plaxton made only minor changes to the Duple design. **2 December 1995**

LEFT: Maidstone & District 2846 a Plaxton Paramount 3500 3 Expressliner on Volvo B10M-60 chassis was acquired from Express Travel of Speke in June 1995. It stands behind Maidstone garage next to 2173 which was new to London Country North East as TP35. **2 December 1995**

ABOVE LEFT: Maidstone & District Bristol VRT 5877 received this all over advertisement livery for the Tesco superstore at Lunsford Park. It is pictured alongside Maidstone garage. **2 December 1995**

ABOVE RIGHT: Two preserved Maidstone & District vehicles in the front yard of Maidstone garage. HKE867 is a 1945 Bristol K6A rebodied in 1953 by Weymann and owned by members of The M&D and East Kent Bus Club, alongside is VKR470 a 1956 AEC Regent V. **2 December 1995**

LEFT: Maidstone & District Leyland Olympian 5931 on route 155 at Chatham station. **19 July 1997**

LEFT: Former Maidstone & District and East Kent 1963 Leyland Atlantean new as 620UKM and latterly operating on the Thanet open top service 69 has now been sold to Guide Friday and as seen here is operating their tour of Portsmouth. **3 August 1997**

LEFT: This former East Kent AEC Regent V MFN944F is seen in a yard near Chepstow believed to be owned by the dealer David Hoare. **4 August 1997**

LEFT: Ex LT DMS2291 was acquired by Maidstone & District from fellow Arriva company Leaside Buses on 24 July specifically to operate the open top tour of Rochester. It was given fleet number 6666 and is at Gillingham about to take up service. Note the traditional fleetname scroll in white. **16 August 1997**

LEFT: Dennis Dart 3213 in the new Maidstone & District livery working on route 114 outside Chatham Pentagon bus station. **16 August 1997**

ABOVE LEFT: Maidstone & District acquired two Dennis Darts following the collapse of the Cardiff Bluebird operation in September 1996 (hence the registration plate) This is the second of the two and is numbered 3475 and is working route 113 outside Chatham Pentagon. **16 August 1997**

ABOVE RIGHT: Maidstone & District coach 2172 was new as LCBS TP14, but was acquired from Kentish Bus in June. It stands near Bexley during a club tour. **16 August 1997**

RIGHT: Maidstone & District service vehicle P43 was new to MOD (Army) as 80 KF 62 it is a Dodge S13/Wadham Stringer driver training bus and is seen over the pits in Maidstone garage. **16 August 1997**

BELOW: These two Van Hool Alizee bodied DAFs operated for Kentish Bus on Green Line work from Northfleet garage. These services passed to London Coaches and the coaches became surplus. J17AMB passed to Maidstone & District and numbered 2197, but was not used, this and K22AMB both passed to New Enterprise. They are seen at Maidstone garage. **16 August 1997**

ABOVE LEFT: A smartly turned out Leyland Lynx. Maidstone & District 3046 was acquired from Shearings in December 1991. It is about to enter the rear of Maidstone garage. **16 August 1997**

ABOVE RIGHT: The rear of Maidstone garage finds Maidstone & District Tiger coach 2196 new to Bebb and New Enterprise Leopard MPL134W which was new to LCBS as DL14. **16 August 1997**

LEFT: Operating a connecting service for the club AGM is preserved East Kent GFN273 a 1952 Beadle-Leyland TD5 outside Heather House Longshaw Road, Maidstone. **29 November 1997**

BELOW LEFT: Also operating a connecting service for the club AGM is preserved 1959 Maidstone & District Park Royal bodied AEC Reliance 277DKT outside Heather House Longshaw Road, Maidstone. **29 November 1997**